BRITANNICA BEGINNER BIOS

ADA LOVELACE
MATHEMATICIAN AND FIRST PROGRAMMER

KRISTI LEW

Britannica
Educational Publishing

IN ASSOCIATION WITH

ROSEN
EDUCATIONAL SERVICES

The John P. Holt Brentwood Library
8109 Concord Road
Brentwood, TN 37027
Phone: 615-371-0090

Published in 2018 by Britannica Educational Publishing (a trademark of Encyclopædia Britannica, Inc.) in association with The Rosen Publishing Group, Inc.
29 East 21st Street, New York, NY 10010

Copyright © 2018 The Rosen Publishing Group, Inc. and Encyclopædia Britannica, Inc. Encyclopædia Britannica, Britannica, and the Thistle logo are registered trademarks of Encyclopædia Britannica, Inc. All rights reserved.

Distributed exclusively by Rosen Publishing.
To see additional Britannica Educational Publishing titles, go to rosenpublishing.com.

First Edition

Britannica Educational Publishing
J.E. Luebering: Executive Director, Core Editorial
Mary Rose McCudden: Editor, Britannica Student Encyclopedia

Rosen Publishing
Kathy Kuhtz Campbell: Senior Editor
Nelson Sá: Art Director
Brian Garvey: Series Designer
Ellina Litmanovich: Book Layout
Cindy Reiman: Photography Manager
Nicole Baker: Photo Researcher

Library of Congress Cataloging-in-Publication Data

Names: Lew, Kristi.
Title: Ada Lovelace: mathematician and first programmer / Kristi Lew.
Description: New York: Britannica Educational Publishing, in Association with Rosen Educational Services, 2018. | Series: Britannica beginner bios | Audience: Grades 1–4. | Includes bibliographical references and index.
Identifiers: LCCN 2017015877 | ISBN 9781680488128 (library bound: alk. paper) | ISBN 9781680488111 (pbk.: alk. paper) | ISBN 9781538300220 (6 pack: alk. paper)
Subjects: LCSH: Lovelace, Ada King, Countess of, 1815–1852—Juvenile literature. | Women mathematicians—Great Britain—Biography—Juvenile literature. | Women computer programmers—Great Britain—Biography—Juvenile literature. | Mathematicians—Great Britain—Biography—Juvenile literature. | Computer programmers—Great Britain—Biography—Juvenile literature.
Classification: LCC QA29.L72 L49 2018 | DDC 510.92 [B] —dc23
LC record available at https://lccn.loc.gov/2017015877

Manufactured in the United States of America

Photo credits: Cover, pp. 1 Universal Images Group/Getty Images; p. 4 Photo 12/Universal Images Group/Getty Images; pp. 5, 16 Art Collection 3/Alamy Stock Photo; pp. 6, 17 Science & Society Picture Library/Getty Images; pp. 8 (left), 10 Hulton Archive/Getty Images; pp. 8 (right), 19 Art Collection/Alamy Stock Photo; p. 9 Culture Club/Hulton Archive/Getty Images; p. 11 Chronicle/Alamy Stock Photo; p. 12 Visuals Unlimited Inc./Robert Pickett/Visuals Unlimited/Getty Images; p. 13 Bettmann/Getty Images; p. 14 National Galleries of Scotland/Hulton Fine Art Collection/Getty Images; p. 16 The Bettmann Archive; p. 18 From Memoir of Augustus De Morgan by Sophia Elizabeth De Morgan, 1882; p. 21 Science Photo Library/Getty Images; p. 22 Ian Francis stock/Alamy Stock Photo; p. 24 vgaijc/E+/Getty Images; p. 26 sabrisy/Shutterstock.com; p. 28 © Imago via Zuma Press.

CONTENTS

Chapter 1
WHO WAS ADA LOVELACE?   4

Chapter 2
A YOUNG MATHEMATICIAN   7

Chapter 3
STUDYING MACHINES   12

Chapter 4
REASON MEETS IMAGINATION   18

Chapter 5
REMEMBERING ADA   24

Timeline   29
Glossary   30
For More Information   31
Index   32

CHAPTER ONE
WHO WAS ADA LOVELACE?

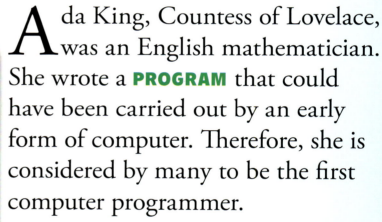

Ada King, Countess of Lovelace, was an English mathematician. She wrote a **PROGRAM** that could have been carried out by an early form of computer. Therefore, she is considered by many to be the first computer programmer.

Computers are machines that work with information. This information can be in the form of

Ada King, Countess of Lovelace, wrote programs for an early form of computer. Her computer programs were the first ones ever to be published.

WHO WAS ADA LOVELACE?

numbers, words, pictures, movies, or sounds. Computer information is also called data. Computers can work with huge amounts of data and produce results very quickly. They also store and display data.

An English inventor and mathematician named Charles Babbage dreamed up the first computer in the 1830s. Babbage's machine did not run on electricity like today's computers because scientists did not yet know how electricity

Charles Babbage developed plans for the first computer in the mid-1830s. He designed it to be able to perform any arithmetic operation.

Vocabulary

A **PROGRAM** is a set of step-by-step instructions that tell a computer to do something with data.

ADA LOVELACE

> **Quick Fact**
>
> In 1855, a Swedish company made a calculator based on Babbage's machine, but the modern electronic computer was not developed until much later.

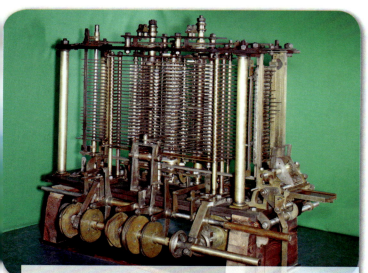

Only a small part of Babbage's computer was built during his lifetime. The machine was designed to follow instructions that people entered using punched cards.

worked. Instead, Babbage's machine called for more than fifty thousand moving parts. It was so complicated that the machine was never constructed during Babbage's lifetime. But it is still considered to be the first computer. Ada Lovelace created a set of commands that would have worked on Babbage's machine had it ever been built.

CHAPTER TWO
A YOUNG MATHEMATICIAN

Ada was born on December 10, 1815, in what is now London, England. Her birth name was Augusta Ada Byron. She was the daughter of the famous poet Lord Byron and Annabella Milbanke Byron. Ada's first name, Augusta, was the name of Lord Byron's half-sister.

Lord Byron's first collection of poetry was made public in 1807, when he was nineteen years old. The long poem that would make him famous was published five years later, in 1812. Almost overnight, the twenty-four-year-old Lord Byron found himself in the spotlight. Byron

ADA LOVELACE

Ada's parents, Lord Byron (*left*) and Anne Isabella (Annabella) Milbanke (*right*), were married in January 1815.

did not handle his fame well. He often acted without any thought to how his deeds might affect other people.

In January 1815, Byron married Anne Isabella (Annabella) Milbanke. The marriage did not last long. Annabella took Ada and left Byron when Ada was just over a month old.

A YOUNG MATHEMATICIAN

> **Quick Fact**
>
> **Annabella, like her daughter, was interested in mathematics and science. Lord Byron called her the "Princess of Parallelograms."**

Byron left England to escape both his debts and the poor public opinion about his behavior. After a number of years, he became interested in Greece's struggle to free itself from Turkish rule. He went to Greece to help with the fight. While he was there, Byron came down with a fever. He died on April 19, 1824. He was thirty-six years old.

Ada was eight when her father died. She never knew him personally. However, at the time, Byron was one

Lord Byron's poetry inspired many artists. This picture was based on a line from his most famous poem.

ADA LOVELACE

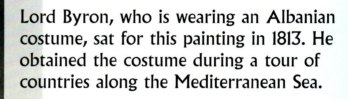

Lord Byron, who is wearing an Albanian costume, sat for this painting in 1813. He obtained the costume during a tour of countries along the Mediterranean Sea.

of the most talked-about men in London society. Ada would never escape the gossip that swirled around him. Nor was she able to get away from the interest people had in her as his only lawful heir.

Lady Byron feared the idea of Ada becoming artistic like her father. Therefore, she did her best to control her daughter's imagination. She also made sure Ada was thoroughly educated in science, logic, and mathematics.

Quick Fact

It was unusual for girls to be educated during Ada's time. However, Lady Byron was wealthy and highly educated herself. These advantages allowed Ada opportunities that other girls did not have.

A YOUNG MATHEMATICIAN

Ada was taught at home by private tutors. She suffered from long periods of poor health. One of the worst illnesses paralyzed her and left her bedridden from early 1829 to the middle of 1832. Some historians have suggested that the illness was measles or **POLIO**. Others have said the sickness was all in Ada's mind. No one really knows exactly what was wrong with her.

> **Vocabulary**
>
> **POLIO** is a disease that affects nerve cells in the spinal cord. It can paralyze someone and make muscle tissue break down. It is caused by a virus and can be spread from one person to another.

Ada's formal education began when she was four years old. A typical day included instruction in arithmetic, music, and French.

CHAPTER THREE
STUDYING MACHINES

As a girl, Ada was fascinated with machines. She was also interested in flying. She studied the wings of birds to find out how they worked. Then she made detailed drawings and built her own pair of wings. She loved riding horses and dreamed of making a steam-powered, horse-shaped flying machine that she could

Ada studied the wings of birds and how they worked so she could make a pair of wings for herself.

STUDYING MACHINES

ride. As she got older, her excitement about flying horses disappeared, but her fascination with machines did not.

In May 1833, seventeen-year-old Ada was introduced to London society. Shortly after, she met Charles Babbage for the first time. Babbage had recently built part of his Difference Engine. The Difference Engine was a huge, mechanical calculator. Its purpose was to make it easier to perform long mathematical calculations. Ada was very interested in Babbage's machine. She asked Babbage for his drawings so she could study them and understand how the machine worked.

Around this time, Ada was introduced to Mary Somerville. Somerville was a British science writer and mathematician. She was

Babbage built the Difference Engine to make it easier to produce accurate calculations.

ADA LOVELACE

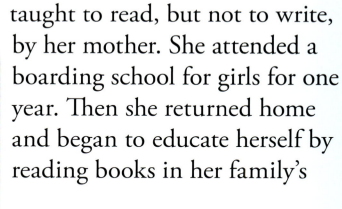

Quick Fact

In 2002, the printing part of Babbage's Difference Engine was finally built from the plans he had made. It worked perfectly. The calculating section had been constructed in 1991.

very good at explaining how different scientific fields fit together. Somerville was an unusual woman for her time. She had very little formal education. She was taught to read, but not to write, by her mother. She attended a boarding school for girls for one year. Then she returned home and began to educate herself by reading books in her family's

Mary Somerville was a wise and faithful teacher and adviser to Ada. Somerville studied mathematics, geography, and astronomy, among other sciences.

STUDYING MACHINES

library. Ada, Somerville, and Somerville's son regularly attended parties at Charles Babbage's house. Somerville's son would become one of Ada's closest friends.

> **Vocabulary**
> A **LOOM** is a machine for weaving threads or yarns to produce cloth.

In the summer of 1834, Ada and her mother went on a tour of manufacturing businesses in northern England. In one of the factories they visited, Ada saw a Jacquard **LOOM**. Where earlier machines could produce only plain cloth, this loom could weave patterns into

> **Quick Fact**
> Babbage and Somerville were not the only people Ada met in London. She also came to know the scientists Charles Darwin and Michael Faraday as well as the writer Charles Dickens.

ADA LOVELACE

A string of punched cards entered the top of a Jacquard loom. The order of holes told the machine how to weave a pattern.

the cloth. Cards of heavy paper with holes punched into them controlled the loom. These punched cards told the loom how to weave the pattern.

Around the time that Ada was touring northern England with her mother, Babbage came up with the plans for another machine. He called this machine the Analytical Engine. It had many of the basic features of a modern computer. Babbage had heard about the Jacquard loom. He was inspired by that machine and

STUDYING MACHINES

planned to use punched cards to enter data into his own machine.

On July 8, 1835, nineteen-year-old Ada married William King. When he became an earl in 1838, she became Countess of Lovelace. The couple had three children. Their oldest son, Byron, was born on May 12, 1836. A daughter, Annabella, was born on September 22, 1837. Their last child, another son, Ralph, was born in July 1839.

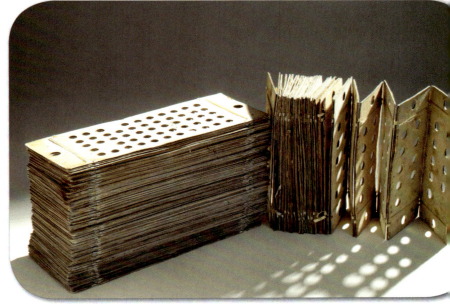

Babbage's idea for his machine was to use a chain of punched cards to control the kind and order of arithmetic operations. The pattern of holes would give the engine specific instructions.

CHAPTER FOUR
REASON MEETS IMAGINATION

By the end of 1839, Lovelace had turned her attention back toward mathematics, and she thought of her friend Babbage. She wrote to him seeking a tutor to help her learn more about mathematics. A tutor is a person who has the responsibility of teaching and guiding another. Babbage was too busy to help her. Lovelace

An important mathematician and logician, Augustus De Morgan was Lovelace's tutor in mathematics.

REASON MEETS IMAGINATION

> **Quick Fact**
>
> **Luigi Federico Menabrea later served as the prime minister, or chief officer of the government, of Italy from 1867 to 1869.**

looked elsewhere and found Augustus De Morgan, a mathematician and logician, who was willing to help further her education.

Late in 1842, Lovelace became aware of a paper about Babbage's Analytical Engine. Luigi Federico Menabrea,

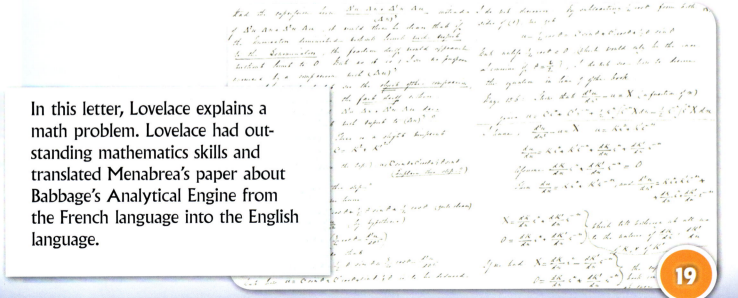

In this letter, Lovelace explains a math problem. Lovelace had outstanding mathematics skills and translated Menabrea's paper about Babbage's Analytical Engine from the French language into the English language.

> **Vocabulary**
>
> **SYMBOLS** are things that stand for something else. For example, musical notes are symbols that stand for certain sounds. They tell musicians what sounds to play and in what order to play them.

a young Italian mathematician and engineer, wrote the paper in French. Lovelace thought more people should know about this new machine. She decided to translate the paper from French into English.

When Lovelace finished her translation, she sent her work to Babbage for his approval. Babbage saw that she had an excellent understanding of the machine and a gift for explaining how it worked. He asked her to add her own ideas to the article. Lovelace decided to do so by adding notes to the end of it. Her notes are more than twice the length of the original article. In her notes, Lovelace explained that there was no reason that a machine such as

REASON MEETS IMAGINATION

Babbage's could not work with anything that could be put into **SYMBOLS**. Symbols include letters, words, musical notes, and numbers. The idea that a machine could work with artistic symbols as well as mathematical ones was a new concept.

Lovelace's notes also contained several programs for the Analytical Engine to carry out. Historians believe it is likely that Babbage wrote instructions for his machine to carry out, too. However, Lovelace's programs were the first to be published.

Like the Jacquard loom, Babbage's machine was controlled by sets of punched

Babbage's son completed part of his father's Analytical Engine in 1910. There were four major parts to the original design: the mill, store, reader, and printer. The mill and printer are shown here.

Lovelace was buried beside her father in the Byron family vault in St. Mary Magdalene Church in Hucknall in 1852.

cards. The pattern of punched holes told the machine which actions it should carry out, when to do so, and in what order. In the case of the loom, the cards told

REASON MEETS IMAGINATION

> **Quick Fact**
>
> In 1839 a picture of Joseph-Marie Jacquard was woven into a piece of silk using the Jacquard loom. It required twenty-four thousand punched cards to tell the loom how to make the picture.

the machine whether or not to raise a piece of yarn. By following the directions programmed by the cards, the loom would weave a pattern in the cloth. With Babbage's machine, the cards held the instructions for carrying out different mathematical operations.

Lovelace's translation of Menabrea's paper, which included her notes, was published in September 1843. Her notes turned out to be the major work of her life. She became sick shortly after finishing them. She died on November 27, 1852. Like her father, she was thirty-six years old at the time of her death.

CHAPTER FIVE
REMEMBERING ADA

Today's computers are electronic devices. This means that they work with electricity. All computer data is carried in tiny flows of electricity called

Students learn how to write computer programs in a coding class.

electric currents. Inside a computer are thousands or millions of tiny electronic parts called transistors. The transistors act as switches. They control how the electric currents flow.

Computers use these electric currents to represent the numbers 0 and 1. Computers use only these two numbers because transistors, like light switches, have only two states—they are either on or off. A transistor that is "on" represents one of the numbers. A transistor that is "off" represents the other. Computers use strings of 0s and 1s to stand for letters, sounds, and all the other data they handle. For example, a computer

Quick Fact

Early computers used punched cards just like Babbage's Analytical Engine. The holes in the cards did the same job that transistors do in modern computers.

stores the word "dog" as three numbers: 01100100 (*d*), 01101111 (*o*), and 01100111 (*g*).

Computers can understand only these patterns of 0s and 1s. All the instructions that a computer follows must be in this form. But people find it hard to work with long number patterns. So, computer programmers have their own special languages. BASIC, Java, and C++ are examples of programming languages. Programmers use these languages to write **ALGORITHMS** for the computer. These step-

Computer code is written in a programming language, such as BASIC, Java, C++, or Ada. Ada is a major programming language for the US defense systems.

REMEMBERING ADA

> **Vocabulary**
>
> **ALGORITHMS** are step-by-step methods for solving a problem or accomplishing a goal.

by-step instructions tell the computer what to do. A computer turns these algorithms into number patterns that it can understand. In 1980, the United States Department of Defense chose Ada as its standard programming language. This language was named for Ada, Countess of Lovelace.

In the early twenty-first century, the second Tuesday in October became Ada Lovelace Day. This is a day that allows people all over the world to honor the work done by women in science, technology, engineering, and mathematics. Ada Lovelace

ADA LOVELACE

Mary Allen Wilkes, a computer pioneer, is seen here holding a computer at an exhibit honoring the two hundredth anniversary of Ada Lovelace's birth. In the 1960s, Wilkes was the first person in the world to build and work on a computer at home.

Day also inspires people to learn more about and to write about women who have advanced scientific knowledge throughout history.

TIMELINE

1815: Lord Byron and Anne Isabella (Annabella) Milbanke marry on January 2.

Augusta Ada Byron is born on December 10.

1816: Annabella takes Ada and leaves Byron in January.

1824: Byron dies on April 19, at the age of thirty-six.

1829: Ada gets sick. She is paralyzed, nearly blind, and has to stay in bed.

1832: Ada finally gets better about midyear.

1833: Ada meets Charles Babbage.

1834: Ada and her mother visit factories in northern England, where Ada sees a Jacquard loom for the first time.

1835: Ada marries William King in July.

1836: The couple's son Byron is born in May.

1837: The couple's daughter, Annabella, is born in September.

1838: William becomes an earl, making Ada the Countess of Lovelace.

1839: Ada and William's third child, their son Ralph, is born in July.

1840: Augustus De Morgan is Ada's tutor.

1842: Luigi Federico Menabrea's paper, describing Babbage's Analytical Engine and written in French, is published in October.

1843: Lovelace's translation of Menabrea's paper into English, along with her notes, is published in September.

1852: Lovelace dies in November at the age of thirty-six.

1991: The London Science Museum builds the calculating part of Babbage's Difference Engine in time for his two hundredth birthday.

2002: The London Science Museum builds the printing part of the Difference Engine for the first time from Babbage's plans.

GLOSSARY

ARTISTIC Showing skill, imagination, and creativity in making things that are beautiful to look at, listen to, or read.

CALCULATOR A device for making mathematical calculations.

CONCEPT An idea or a thought.

DATA Information that can be used in calculating, reasoning, or planning.

DEBT Owing something to someone.

EARL A member of the British nobility.

ELECTRICITY A form of energy produced by the movement of charged particles.

ELECTRONIC Of or related to flowing electrons, or electricity.

HEIR A person who inherits or has the right to inherit a title or the property of someone who dies.

LOGIC The study of the rules and tests of sound reasoning.

LOGICIAN One who is skilled or trained in the processes used in thinking and reasoning.

MATHEMATICAL OPERATION The process of adding, subtracting, multiplying, dividing, or otherwise working with numbers.

MATHEMATICS The science of numbers and their properties, relationships, and measurement. An expert in mathematics is called a mathematician.

PARALYZED Unable to move or feel all or part of the body.

POET A person who writes poetry.

PUBLISHED Made something known to the public, usually in written form, such as when a book is printed.

REPRESENT To take the place of something else.

WEAVE To form fabric by lacing threads going lengthwise together with threads going crosswise.

FOR MORE INFORMATION

BOOKS

Bodden, Valerie. *Programming Pioneer Ada Lovelace* (STEM Trailblazer Bios). Minneapolis, MN: Lerner Publications, 2017.

Hayes, Amy. *Ada Lovelace: First Computer Programmer* (Computer Pioneers). New York, NY: PowerKids Press, 2017.

Labrecque, Ellen. *Ada Lovelace and Computer Algorithms* (Women Innovators). Ann Arbor, MI: Cherry Lake Publishing, 2017.

Robinson, Fiona. *Ada's Ideas: The Story of Ada Lovelace, the World's First Computer Programmer*. New York, NY: Abrams Books for Young Readers, 2016.

Stanley, Diane. *Ada Lovelace, Poet of Science: The First Computer Programmer*. New York, NY: Simon & Schuster/Paula Wiseman Books, 2016.

WEBSITES

Because of the changing nature of internet links, Rosen Publishing has developed an online list of websites related to the subject of this book. This site is updated regularly. Please use this link to access the list:

http://www.rosenlinks.com/BBB/Lovelace

INDEX

Ada (language), 27
Ada Lovelace Day, 27–28
algorithms, 26–27
Analytical Engine, 16, 19–21, 25

Babbage, Charles, 5–6, 13, 15–16, 18–21
Byron, Annabella Milbanke (mother), 7, 8, 10
Byron, Lord (father), 7–10

childhood, 7–11
children, 17

data, 5, 17, 24–25
death, 23
DeMorgan, Augustus, 19
Department of Defense, 27
Difference Engine, 13

education, 10–11
electricity, 5, 24–25

Jacquard loom, 15–16, 21–23

King, William, 17

legacy, 27–28

marriage, 17
Menabrea, Luigi Federico, 19–20, 23

polio, 11
program, 4
programming languages, 26–27
punched cards, 16–17, 21–23, 25

Somerville, Mary, 13–15
symbols, 21